EARTH SCIENCE—LANDFORMS Need to Know

SilverTip

Plains

by Ashley Kuehl

Consultant: Jordan Stoleru,
Science Educator

BEARPORT
PUBLISHING

Minneapolis, Minnesota

Credits

Cover and title page, © Maxim Khytra/AdobeStock; 3, © Ruslan Suseynov/Shutterstock , 5T, © Creative Travel Projects/Shutterstock; 5M, © Viktollio/Shutterstock; 5B, © Andrei Stepanov/Shutterstock; 7, © marekuliasz/iStock; 9T, © Evgeniy Andreev/iStock; 9B, © maradon 333/Shutterstock; 10–11, © Simon Dannhauer/Shutterstock; 11, © Adelclos/Shutterstock; 13, © Max Lindenthaler/Shutterstock; 14–15, © stammphoto/iStock; 17, © Phoenixproduction/iStock; 18, © lembi/Shutterstock; 19, © EcoPrint/Shutterstock; 21, © volkova natalia/Shutterstock; 22, © Cristian Lourenço/iStock; 23, © Ultima_Gaina/iStock; 25, © Bilanol/Shutterstock; 26, © PhotoQuest/Getty Images; 27, © Peteri/Shutterstock; 28B , © Platon Anton/Shutterstock.

Bearport Publishing Company Product Development Team

President: Jen Jenson; Director of Product Development: Spencer Brinker; Managing Editor: Allison Juda; Associate Editor: Naomi Reich; Associate Editor: Tiana Tran; Art Director: Colin O'Dea; Designer: Kim Jones; Designer: Kayla Eggert; Product Development Assistant: Owen Hamlin

Statement on Usage of Generative Artificial Intelligence

Bearport Publishing remains committed to publishing high-quality nonfiction books. Therefore, we restrict the use of generative AI to ensure accuracy of all text and visual components pertaining to a book's subject. See BearportPublishing.com for details.

Library of Congress Cataloging-in-Publication Data

Names: Kuehl, Ashley, 1977- author.
Title: Plains / by Ashley Kuehl.
Description: Minneapolis, Minnesota: Bearport Publishing Company, 2025. | Series: Earth science. Landforms : need to know | Includes bibliographical references and index.
Identifiers: LCCN 2024006089 (print) | LCCN 2024006090 (ebook) | ISBN 9798892320511 (library binding) | ISBN 9798892325257 (paperback) | ISBN 9798892321846 (ebook)
Subjects: LCSH: Plains–Juvenile literature.
Classification: LCC GB572 .K84 2025 (print) | LCC GB572 (ebook) | DDC 551.45/3–dc23/eng/20240215
LC record available at https://lccn.loc.gov/2024006089
LC ebook record available at https://lccn.loc.gov/2024006090

Copyright © 2025 Bearport Publishing Company. All rights reserved. No part of this publication may be reproduced in whole or in part, stored in any retrieval system, or transmitted in any form or by any means, electronic, mechanical, photocopying, recording, or otherwise, without written permission from the publisher. Bearport Publishing is a division of Chrysalis Education Group.

For more information, write to Bearport Publishing, 5357 Penn Avenue South, Minneapolis, MN 55419.

Contents

The Flattest Landform 4
Plain Plains 6
Grassland Plains 8
Cold, Hot, and Very Wet 12
Lava Plains 16
Breaking Off and Washing Away . . 18
Rivers Move Sediment 20
People Need Plains 24

How Rivers Form Plains 28
SilverTips for Success 29
Glossary 30
Read More 31
Learn More Online 31
Index 32
About the Author 32

The Flattest Landform

What does a stretch of rolling, grassy hills have in common with a flat, sandy desert? It's the same thing they both share with a flat, treeless area at the top of a mountain. These places are all types of plains.

> Plains are one of Earth's major **landforms**. They can be found on every continent. Plains cover about a third of Earth's land.

Plain Plains

Plains may look different, but they are all mostly level. This flatness is what they share in common.

Plains can be almost any size. The smallest takes up less than a square mile of land. The largest is more than a million square miles (3 million sq km).

> The biggest plains area in North America is the Great Plains. This landform touches 10 different states, as well as parts of Canada.

The Great Plains

Grassland Plains

Plains look different in different places. They can be found in different climates. Many have grasslands. They grow grasses but have few trees.

A temperate grassland has cold winters and hot summers. In North America, these grasslands are called prairies. They are called steppes (STEPS) in central Europe and Asia.

> Prairies and steppes are a lot alike. However, prairies get more rain. This makes it possible for more plants to grow there. Steppes usually have shorter grasses and fewer kinds of plants.

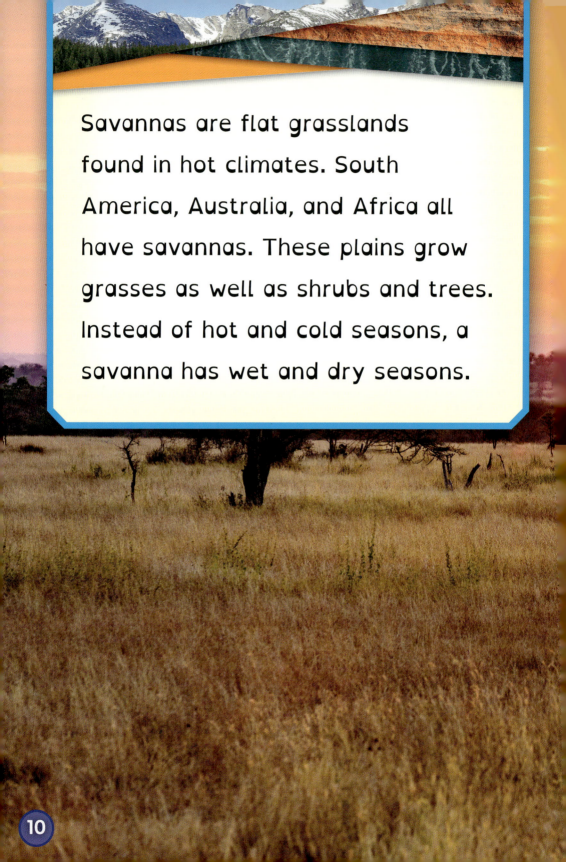

Savannas are flat grasslands found in hot climates. South America, Australia, and Africa all have savannas. These plains grow grasses as well as shrubs and trees. Instead of hot and cold seasons, a savanna has wet and dry seasons.

It is easy to see far and wide on the savanna. This makes prey animals easier to spot. Many use **camouflage** to stay safe out in the open.

Cold, Hot, and Very Wet

Some plains are cold and dry. They are called tundras. The word *tundra* means treeless plain. Because the ground is frozen and there is so little rain, few plants grow.

Plains in the **Arctic** are tundras. Tundras are also found at the tops of some mountains.

> Tundras are cold deserts. Hot deserts can cover plains, too. Their land is flat and dry. Very few plants grow in hot or cold deserts.

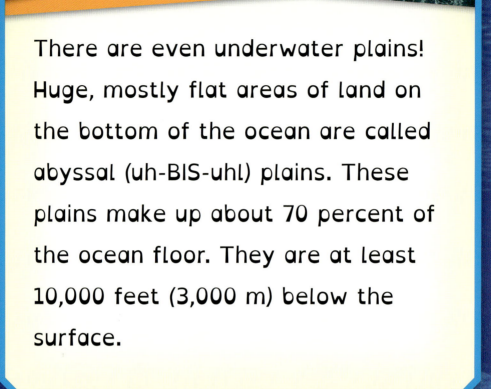

There are even underwater plains! Huge, mostly flat areas of land on the bottom of the ocean are called abyssal (uh-BIS-uhl) plains. These plains make up about 70 percent of the ocean floor. They are at least 10,000 feet (3,000 m) below the surface.

Plains are found along the ocean floor all around the world. But the Atlantic Ocean has more of these plains than any other ocean.

Lava Plains

Plains can form in a few ways. Some plains were made from lava. This superhot liquid rock sometimes flows up from underground through cracks in Earth's crust. Above ground, the lava may spread for miles. As it cools, this lava can flatten into a plain.

Plains made from lava are sometimes called lava plains. They are also called lava fields. Their rocky surfaces are usually darker in color than other plains.

Breaking Off and Washing Away

Some plains are formed as other landforms wear away. Wind, water, or ice can break off tiny bits of the land. This is called **weathering**. Then, a process called **erosion** carries away the tiny pieces known as **sediment**. What is left behind is flattened land.

Glaciers can also change landforms. These huge sheets of ice are always slowly moving. As they do, they can move sediment from one place to another. This leaves plains behind.

Rivers Move Sediment

Adding sediment to an area can also make plains. Plains often form around rivers near mountains. As mountain snow melts, it picks up sediment. The snowmelt flows into rivers. This can cause flooding, sending water and sediment onto land around the river. The sediment stays even after the water goes away.

> Rivers can cause weathering and erosion, too. Flowing water may break off pieces of land from one place. Then, it drops the sediment in another.

Sometimes, rivers carry sediment all the way to the ocean. The river water **deposits** some of the sediment onto land near the water. This sediment can build up at the coast like it does along riverbanks. It leaves behind flat plains.

The flat area along a coast is called a coastal plain. It can be on land or in the water. An underwater coastal plain is also called a continental shelf.

People Need Plains

Plains are important to humans. They are good for farming. The soil in many plains has a lot of the nutrients plants need. Crops can grow faster and stronger in this soil. The flat land also makes it easier for farmers to plant and gather crops.

Plains made by flooding often have soil that is especially good for growth. That's because floodwater brings nutrients to land along with the sediment.

Many people settle on plains. They build their homes and towns there. In addition to being good for growing food, it is easy to build on and travel across the flat landforms.

Though they are flat, plains are far from plain. These landforms help shape life on Earth.

By the 1930s, harmful farming had hurt the Great Plains. Dust blew the dry soil. Crops wouldn't grow. People were forced to leave their homes. This made people start to take better care of these important landforms.

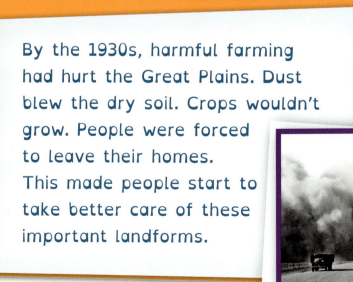

How Rivers Form Plains

Rushing rivers can help form plains in a couple of different ways.

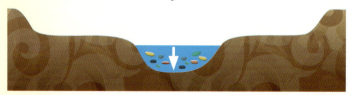

Water carries sediment down a river.

When the river floods, sediment builds up on the land, forming a plain.

The river also carries sediment to the ocean. The sediment collects on the land at the end of the river. Over time, this forms a coastal plain.

SilverTips for SUCCESS

★ SilverTips for REVIEW

Review what you've learned. Use the text to help you.

Define key terms

erosion
grassland
sediment
tundra
weathering

Check for understanding

What are the key features of a plain?

Describe how erosion can change land to create plains.

Explain how lava can form plains.

Think deeper

What is the surface of Earth like where you live? If the landforms around you were different, how might your life be different?

★ SilverTips on TEST-TAKING

- **Make a study plan.** Ask your teacher what the test is going to cover. Then, set aside time to study a little bit every day.

- **Read all the questions carefully.** Be sure you know what is being asked.

- **Skip any questions** you don't know how to answer right away. Mark them and come back later if you have time.

Glossary

Arctic the northernmost area on Earth

camouflage colors and markings on an animal's body that help it blend in with its surroundings

climates patterns of weather in an area over a long period of time

deposits lets things fall or leaves them behind somewhere

erosion the carrying away of rock and soil by natural forces, such as water and wind

landforms natural features on Earth's surface

lava hot rock that comes out of cracks in Earth's surface

nutrients substances needed by plants to grow and stay healthy

sediment tiny pieces of rock that have broken away from larger rocks

temperate a climate with different seasons and few weather extremes compared to hot or cold climates

weathering the breaking apart or wearing away of rock and soil by natural forces, such as water and wind

Read More

Bergin, Raymond. *Grassland Life Connections (Life on Earth! Biodiversity Explained).* Minneapolis: Bearport Publishing Company, 2023.

DK. *Planet Earth! Our Exciting World As You've Never Seen It Before (DK Knowledge Encyclopedia).* New York: DK Publishing, 2022.

Idzikowski, Lisa. *Changing Plains Environments (Human Impact on Earth: Cause and Effect).* New York: PowerKids Press, 2020.

Learn More Online

1. Go to **www.factsurfer.com** or scan the QR code below.
2. Enter "**Plains**" into the search box.
3. Click on the cover of this book to see a list of websites.

Index

abyssal plains 14
climate 8, 10
coastal plains 22, 28
erosion 18, 20
farming 24, 26
grasslands 8, 10
Great Plains, the 6–7, 26
lava plains 16

prairies 8–9
rivers 20, 22, 28
savannas 10–11
sediment 18, 20, 22, 24, 28
steppes 8–9
tundras 12
weathering 18, 20

About the Author

Ashley Kuehl is an editor and writer specializing in nonfiction for young people. She lives in Minneapolis, MN.